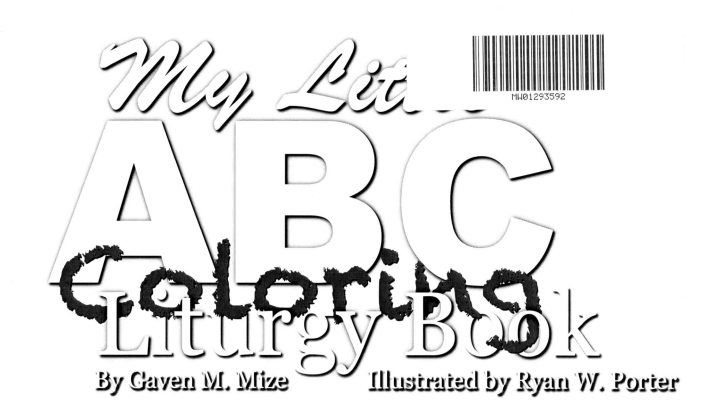

My Little ABC Coloring Liturgy Book

By Gaven M. Mize

Illustrated by Ryan W. Porter

GRAIL QUEST BOOKS + BANGOR

Publisher
Kasandra M. Radke

AUTHOR
© 2017 Gaven M. Mize
All Rights Reserved.

ART, COVER AND LAYOUT
© 2017 Ryan W. Porter
All Rights Reserved.

The quoted texts on the pages pertaining letters G, H, M, N, R, S, T, Z and St. John's Prayer were taken from the Book of Common Prayer (1789), which is in Public Domain.

PUBLICATION HISTORY
Coloring Edition / March 2018
ISBN-13: 978-1-9858911-8-0

MY LITTLE ABC LITURGY COLORING BOOK

PRINTED IN THE UNITED STATES OF AMERICA
1357908642

Grail Quest Books can be found online at
http://www.grailquestbooks.com

Other works of Rev. Gaven M. Mize can be found at
http://www.mizefamilybooks.com

Author Dedications

For my Godchildren:
Jonah Lehman
&
Harper Mize

For my son's Godparents:
Joshua and Tuesday Mize
(Harper and Quinn)
&
Adam and Mandee Mann
(Joshua, Miles, and Lucy)

For the faithful children of
Augustana Evangelical
Lutheran Church
Hickory, North Carolina

Illustrator Dedications

For my Godson:
Alec Ryan Rehorst

For my Sons:
Gryffon Schultz
William Porter
Noah Porter

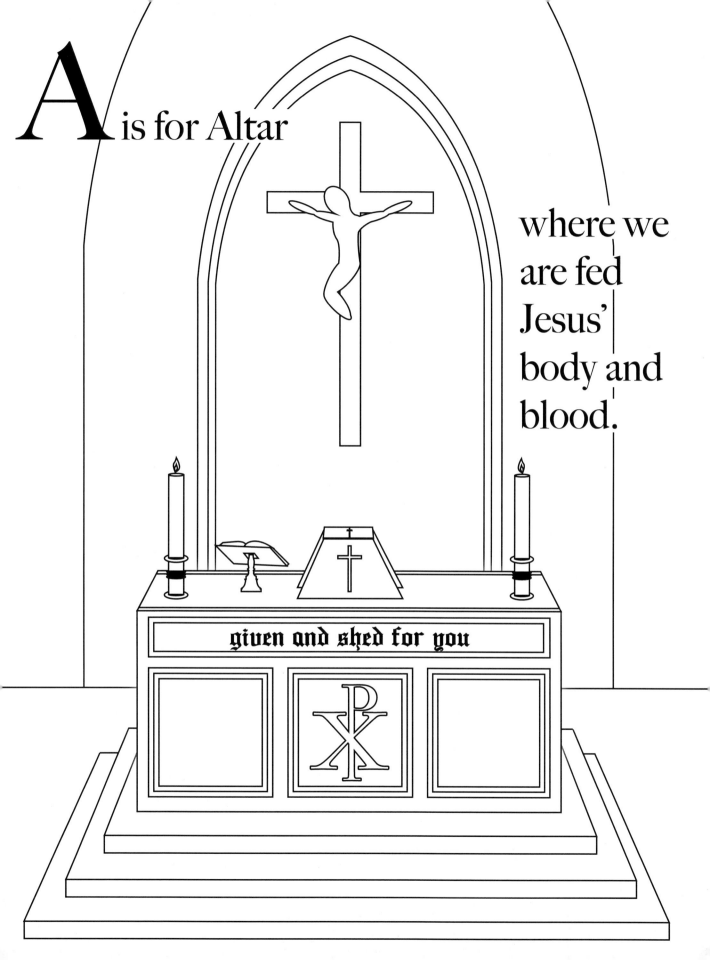

A is for Altar

where we
are fed
Jesus'
body and
blood.

given and shed for you

B is for Baptism

where I
was saved
by water
and word.

given and shed for you

C is for Chasuble

that my Pastor wears at the Altar.

The Chasuble is the outermost vestment used by the pastor who is presiding over the Service of the Sacrament. The Chasuble received its name from the Latin word, "Casula," which means "little house." This poncho like vestment is worn as a Eucharistic (Holy Communion) vestment and highlights the office rather than the man wearing it.

given and shed for you

E is for Eucharist

**Eucharist is the Greek word for thanksgiving.
It is the word that is often used to refer to the Lord's body and blood.
The term Eucharist is derived from Jesus' words of institution in
1 Corinthians 11:23-25**

that is the body and blood of Christ.

IHS

given and shed for you

F is for Frankincense

that smells so sweet to the Lord.

Frankincense is a sweet smelling incense that is burned with a hot coal to allow the incense to melt and give off its unforgettable aroma.

Frankincense is also one of the three gifts brought by the wise men to baby Jesus around the time of His birth.

given and shed for you

G is for the Gloria

when we get to sing praises to our God!

"Glory be to God on high, and on earth peace, good will towards men. We praise thee, we bless thee, we worship thee, we glorify thee, we give thanks to thee for thy great glory, O Lord God, heavenly King, God the Father Almighty. O Lord, the only-begotten Son, Jesus Christ; O Lord God, Lamb of God, Son of the Father, that takest away the sins of the world, have mercy upon us. Thou that takest away the sins of the world, receive our prayer."

"Thou that sittest at the right hand of God the Father, have mercy upon us. For thou only art holy, thou only art the Lord, thou only, O Christ, with the Holy Ghost, art most high in the glory of God the Father Amen."

GLORIA IN EXCELSIS

H is for Hosanna

where we cry to be saved.

Hosanna, in the highest.
Blessed is he
that commeth
in the name of the Lord:
Glory to thee,
O lord in the highest.

HOSANNA IN THE HIGHEST

I is for Invocation when we make the sign of the Cross to remember our baptism.

J is for
JESUS

Who is in
every word
of the Liturgy

DIVINE SERVICE
So faith comes from hearing,

SETTING III
and hearing through the word of Christ

K is for Kyrie Eleison

the Lord has mercy on me.

Lord have mercy,
Christ have mercy,
Lord have mercy.

KYRIE

ELEISON

L is for Liturgy

where we worship the Lord.

GO IN PEACE

M is for Magnificat

Magnificat

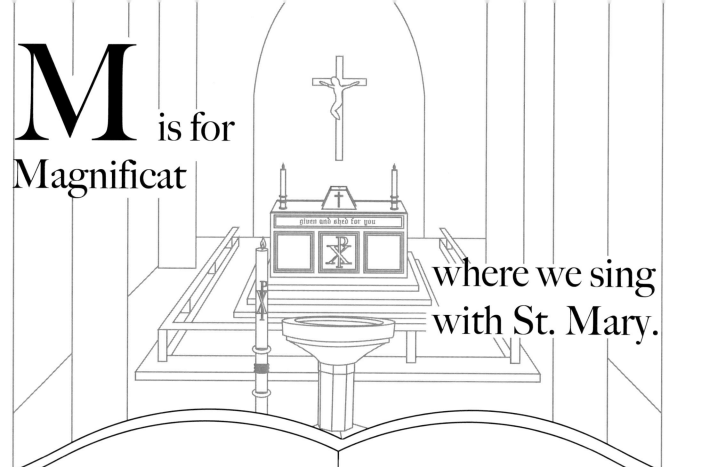

where we sing
with St. Mary.

"My soul doth magnify the Lord,
and my spirit hath rejoiced
in God my Savior.
For he hath regarded
the lowliness of his handmaiden.
For behold from henceforth
all generations shall call me blessed.
For he that is mighty
hath magnified me,
and holy is his Name.
And his mercy is on them that fear him
throughout all generations.
He hath showed strength with his arm;
he hath scattered the proud
in the imagination of their hearts."

"He hath put down the mighty
from their seat,
and hath exalted the humble and meek.
He hath filled the hungry
with good things,
and the rich he hath sent empty away.
He remembering his mercy
hath helped his servant Israel,
as he promised to our forefathers,
Abraham and his seed for ever. "
-Luke 1:46-55

"Glory to the Father, and to the Son,
and to the Holy Spirit:
as it was in the beginning,
is now, and will be forever.
Amen."

Μαριάμ

Θεοτόκος

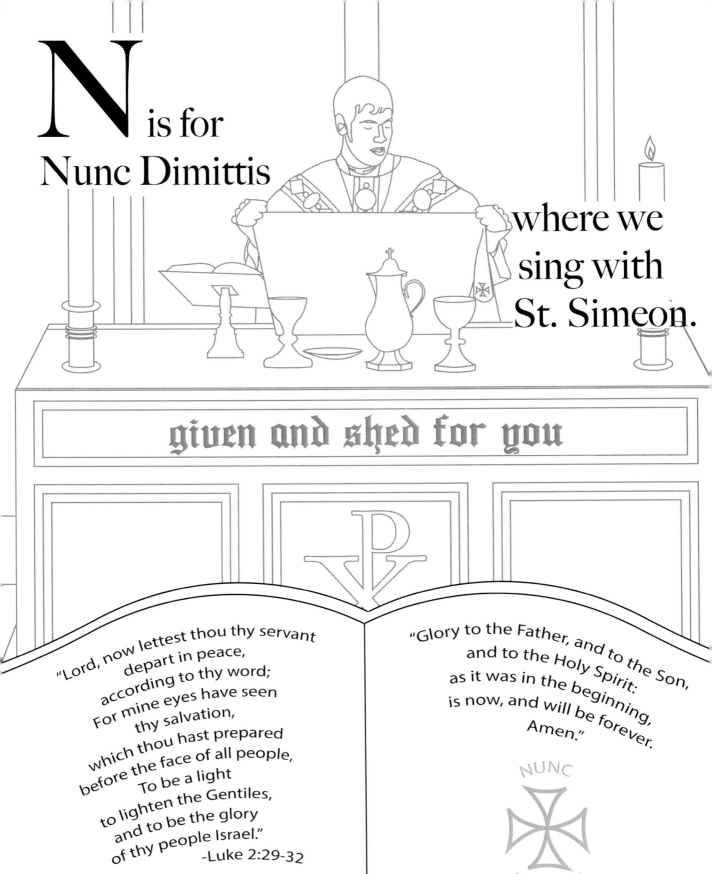

N is for Nunc Dimittis

where we sing with St. Simeon.

given and shed for you

"Lord, now lettest thou thy servant depart in peace, according to thy word; For mine eyes have seen thy salvation, which thou hast prepared before the face of all people, To be a light to lighten the Gentiles, and to be the glory of thy people Israel."
-Luke 2:29-32

"Glory to the Father, and to the Son, and to the Holy Spirit: as it was in the beginning, is now, and will be forever. Amen."

NUNC DIMITTIS

O is for Offering when we give to the church and sing.

given and shed for you

P is for
Pax Domini

which is the peace
of the Lord, and
is the peace of
the Eucharist.

given and shed for you

Q is for Quietness
in the Lord's House
where reverence
is shown.

R is for Rubric

the red words that tell Pastor what to do.

given and shed for yo

P X

P X

The Gospel is read:

P: This is the Gospel of the Lord.
C: Praise to Thee, O Christ.

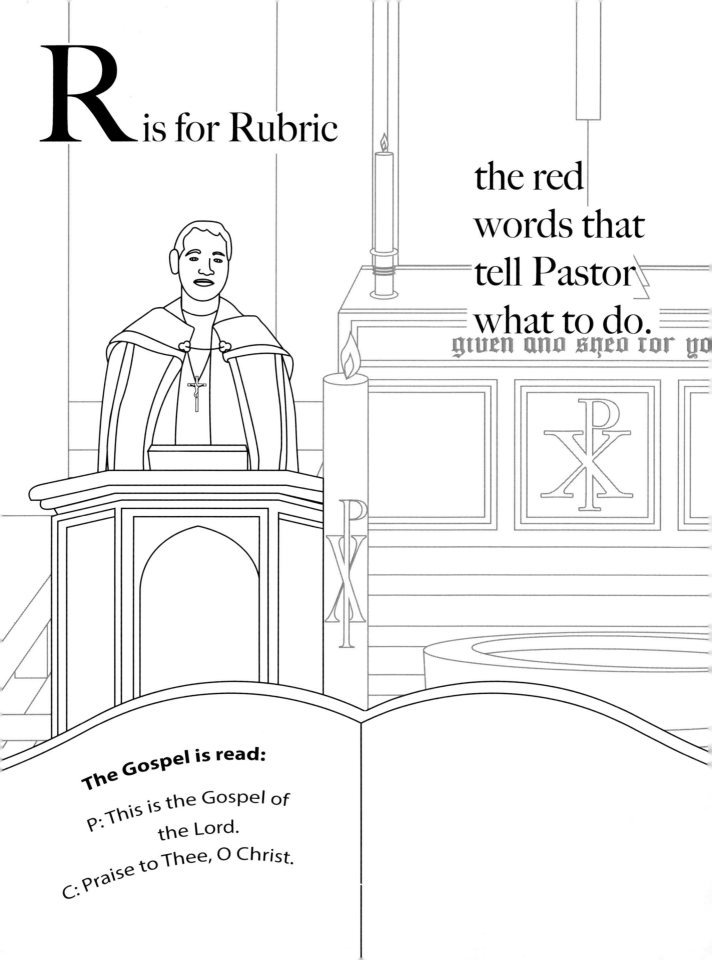

S is for Sanctus

where we sing that God is Holy.

given and shed for you

"Holy, holy, holy, Lord God of Hosts: heaven and earth are full of thy glory: Hosanna, in the highest. Blessed is he that commeth in the name of the Lord: Glory to thee, O Lord in the highest."

HOLY HOLY

HOLY

T is for Te Deum

where we praise God in song.

"We praise thee, O God;
we acknowledge thee to be the Lord.
All the earth doth worship thee,
the Father everlasting.
To thee all Angels cry aloud,
the Heavens and all the Powers therein.
To thee Cherubim and Seraphim
continually do cry:
Holy, holy, holy, Lord God of Sabaoth;
Heaven and earth are full
of the majesty of thy glory.
The glorious company of the apostles
praise thee.
The goodly fellowship of the prophets
praise thee.
The noble army of martyrs praise thee.
The holy Church throughout all the world
doth acknowledge thee,
the Father, of an infinite majesty,
"thine adorable, true, and only Son,"

also the Holy Ghost the Comforter.
Thou art the King of glory, O Christ.
Thou art the everlasting Son of the Father.
When thou tookest upon thee to deliver man,
thou didst humble thyself
to be born of a Virgin.
When thou hadst overcome
the sharpness of death,
thou didst open the kingdom of heaven
to all believers.
Thou sittest at the right hand of God,
in the glory of the Father.
We believe that thou shalt come
to be our judge.
We therefore pray thee, help thy servants,
whom thou hast redeemed
with thy precious blood.
Make them to be numbered
with thy saints,
in glory everlasting."

U is for the Undershepherd

God gave me in my very own Pastor.

V is for the Vestments

put on before the Liturgy.

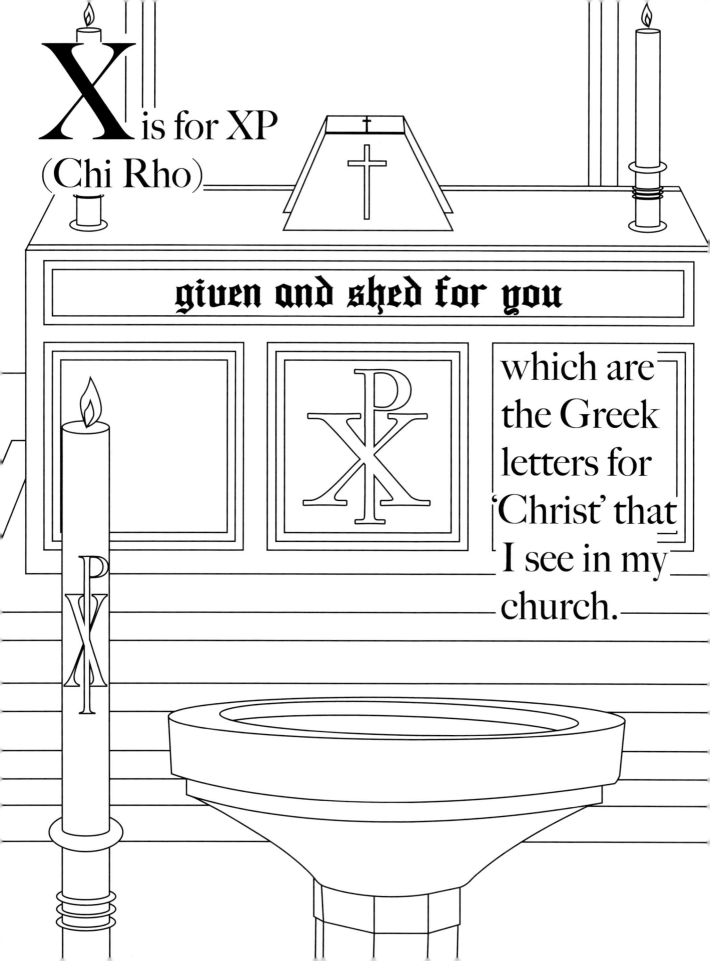

X is for XP
(Chi Rho)

given and shed for you

which are the Greek letters for 'Christ' that I see in my church.

Y is for Yoke (or Stole) to remind my pastor of his role.

given an

Z is for Zachariah's Canticle (Benedictus)

where we Blessed the God of Isreal!

"Blessed be the Lord God of Israel,
for he hath visited and redeemed his people;
And hath raised up a mighty salvation for us
in the house of his servant David,
As he spake by the mouth of his holy prophets,
which have been since the world began:
That we should be saved from our enemies,
and from the hand of all that hate us;
To perform the mercy promised to our forefathers,
and to remember his holy covenant;
To perform the oath which he swore
to our forefather Abraham, that he would give us,
That we being delivered
out of the hand of our enemies
In holiness and righteousness before him,
all the days of our life.
And thou, child, shalt be called"

"the prophet of the Highest,
for thou shalt go before the face of the Lord
to prepare his ways;
To give knowledge of salvation unto his people
for the remission of their sins,
Through the tender mercy of our God,
whereby the dayspring from on high
hath visited us;
To give light to them that sit in darkness
and in the shadow of death,
and to guide our feet into the way of peace.
Glory to the Father, and to the Son,
and to the Holy Spirit:
as it was in the beginning, is now,
and will be for ever. Amen."

Prayer of St. John Chrysostom

Almighty God, who hast given us grace at this time with one accord to make our common supplication unto thee, and hast promised through thy well-beloved Son that when two or three are gathered together in his Name thou wilt be in the midst of them: Fulfill now, O Lord, the desires and petitions of thy servants as may be best for us; granting u in this world knowledge of thy truth, and in the world to come life everlasting. Amen.

About the Author

The Rev. Gaven M. Mize is honored to be the pastor of Augustana Evangelical Lutheran Church in Hickory, North Carolina. He is the husband of Ashlee and father of Oliver Augustine. Rev. Mize hopes that by utilizing liturgical materials during formative years the little ones will grow in faith, wisdom, and in the love of the Divine Service where Christ's greatest gifts are given.

About the Illustrator

Ryan Porter is currently a Graphic Design student at Northeast Wisconsin Technical College. Upon completing his degree, he plans to attend Concordia Theological Seminary in Fort Wayne Indiana; in hopes of entering into the Pastoral Office. He is the husband of Tawny and father of Gryffon, William, and Noah. He was delighted to work on this book with Rev. Mize, in order to help raise his children into the faith that was once for all delivered to the saints.

Manufactured by Amazon.ca
Acheson, AB

13333754R00020